Revive the City

A Booklet to Ignite Citywide Revival

By Dr. Steve Mbua

A Prayer For Our City

"Ask ye of the Lord rain in the time of the latter rain; so the Lord shall make bright clouds, and give them showers of rain, to every one grass in the field."

- Zechariah 10: 1

We are living in the time of the latter rain. Now is the moment to cry out for showers of revival. As Zechariah 10:1 urges us, we must ask boldly and expect God to pour out His Spirit on our cities.

Prayer: Dear Father in heaven, out of City Revival Church in Salado, TX, we pray that people will come to know Jesus, be filled with the Holy Spirit, and that supernatural ministry will take place. We believe that as CRC hosts the presence of God, it will produce a perpetual move of the Spirit that will transform and activate gifts in people for the advancement of the kingdom of God, as the Holy Spirit leads.

Unless otherwise indicated all Scripture quotations are taken from the King James Version of the Bible.

Revive the City

ISBN: 979-8-9904267-5-7

Copyright at 2025 by Dr. Steve Mbua

Printed and bound in U.S.A. All rights reserved under International Copyright Law. Contents and/or cover may not be reproduced in whole or part in any form without the express written consent of the author.

Invest in the Gospel at:

- Wesbite: https://www.cityrevive.org/give/
- Cash App: https://cash.app/$ciicus
- Paypal: https://www.paypal.com/paypalme/ciicdonate
- Thank you for your generosity. Please make checks payable to CRC and mail your gift to: 17701 FM 2115, Salado, TX 76571
- If you want to become a Partner with our ministry, please email pa@cityrevive.org or go@cityrevive.org

Table of Contents

Chapter 1

What Is Revival?..............................6

Chapter 2

Revival Starts with You 7

Chapter 3

Build the Prayer Fire................ Error! Bookmark not defined.

Chapter 4

Unite the Church in Your City...... 11

Chapter 5

Evangelize Boldly 13

Chapter 6

Sustain the Move of God...............15

Chapter 7

Sample Prayers for City Revival.... 17

Chapter 8

You Are a Revival Carrier.............. 21

Chapter 9

Step-by-Step Guide For Revival... 23

Chapter 10

Revival Prayer Guide..................... 31

Chapter 11

City Revival Plan 40

Author Note 48

Notes 54

Notes 55

Chapter 1

What Is Revival?

Revival is when **God's presence comes down** and transforms hearts, homes, churches, and entire regions. It is not just a series of emotional church meetings—it is a **divine awakening** that shakes people out of spiritual slumber and into passionate pursuit of God.

In true revival:
- Sinners are saved.
- Believers are purified and empowered.
- Families are restored.
- Cities feel the impact of Heaven touching earth.

Scripture Focus:

"Will You not revive us again, that Your people may rejoice in You?"
— Psalm 85:6

Chapter 2

Revival Starts With You

Before revival can shake a city, it must first **ignite your soul**.

Revival doesn't begin on a platform or in a stadium — it begins in **private surrender**, with one heart fully yielded to God. If you want to see real transformation in your church, in your neighborhood, and in your nation, it must begin with a fire burning within **you**.

Ask Yourself:
- Am I hungry for more of God?
- Is there any area in me that needs repentance?
- Am I available for God to use?

Scripture Focus:

"Search me, O God, and know my heart; test me and know my anxious thoughts."
— Psalm 139:23

Prayer Declaration:
"Lord, revive me. Make me a vessel of Your glory in my city. Let Your fire burn
Prayer Declaration:
"Lord, revive me. Make me a vessel of Your glory in my city. Let Your fire burn in me until it touches everyone around me."

Chapter 3

Build the Prayer Fire

Every revival in history was **born in prayer**. When God finds people who are willing to cry out, Heaven responds with power.

Prayer is not just a warm-up — it is the **furnace** where the fire of revival is kindled and sustained. If we want to see God move in our city, we must become people who **know how to kneel before we lead**.

How to Build the Fire:
- Start a small prayer group, even with just two or three people.
- Set a consistent time and place for intercession.
- Walk through your city and pray over schools, churches, neighborhoods, and local leaders.
- Fast regularly as God leads.
- Use Scriptures in your prayers — **speak His Word back to Him**.

Scripture Focus:

"If My people, who are called by My name, will humble themselves and pray and seek My face and turn from their wicked ways, then I will hear from heaven..."
— 2 Chronicles 7:14

Prayer Declaration:
"Lord, let the fire on the altar of prayer never go out. Stir us to pray until Heaven opens and revival falls."

Chapter 4

Unite the Church in Your City

Revival cannot be carried by one person or one church alone.

God is looking for a united Body, not isolated ministries. When churches come together in humility and honor, God commands His blessing over the city.

Division weakens our impact, but **unity multiplies our influence.** It's not about who leads — it's about who hosts His presence together.

How to Pursue Unity:
- Reach out to pastors and leaders with a heart, not an agenda.
- Invite other churches to join in prayer gatherings or outreach events.

- Host citywide worship nights where **Jesus is the focus**, not denominations.
- Avoid competition. Celebrate what God is doing in others.

Scripture Focus:

"How good and pleasant it is when God's people live together in unity... For there the Lord commands the blessing."
— Psalm 133:1,3

Prayer Declaration:
"Lord, heal division in Your Church. Break the walls between ministries, races, and generations. Let Your people rise as one voice — let hunger for Your glory grow."

Chapter 5

Evangelize Boldly

Revival is not just for the church — it's for the harvest. When God moves, He moves outward, drawing the lost into the light of His love. It's time to leave the comfort of pews and carry the Gospel into the streets, schools, parks, and marketplaces.

The early Church turned cities upside down not through events, but through **bold, Spirit-filled evangelism**.

How to Evangelize Boldly:
- Share your testimony — your story is powerful.
- Host street outreaches with music, prayer, and free resources.
- Visit hospitals, schools, prisons, and shelters with the love of Jesus.
- Offer healing, prayer and the message of salvation openly and with compassion.

- Train believers in your church to confidently lead others to Christ.

Scripture Focus:

"Go into all the world and preach the Gospel to every creature."
— Mark 16:15

"The righteous are as bold as a lion."
— Proverbs 28:1

Prayer Declaration:

"Lord, give me boldness to proclaim Your Gospel. Let signs and wonders follow as I preach. Use me to bring lost sons and daughters back to You."

Chapter 6

Sustain the Move of God

Revival is not just about a **moment** — it's about building a **movement**. What starts with fire must be sustained with **faithfulness**. Many revivals have began strong but fade because there's no plan to nurture the flames.

God doesn't just want to visit your city — He wants to **dwell there**. That means we must create rhythms, structures, and discipleship paths to keep the fire burning.

How to Sustain the Move:
- Hold weekly revival nights or prayer gatherings.
- Immediately disciple new believers — don't let them fall through the cracks.
- Train and release young leaders to carry the fire.
- Continue fasting and interceding for deeper impact.

- Stay humble — always give God the glory.

Scripture Focus:

"Do not put out the Spirit's fire."
— 1 Thessalonians 5:19

"Fan into flame the gift of God…"
— 2 Timothy 1:6

Prayer Declaration:

"Lord, help us not just spark a revival — but steward it. Teach us to build altars where Your presence remains and generations are transformed."

Chapter 7

Sample Prayers for City Revival

Prayer is the engine of revival. When believers come into agreement with God's heart, cities can be shaken, families can be restored, and entire communities can be transformed.

Use these sample prayers in your prayer meetings, personal devotion, or citywide gatherings. Let them stir your spirit and give voice to your hunger for a move of God.

Prayer for Personal Revival

Scriptures Focus:
Psalm 139:23-14, Psalm 51:10

"Lord, search my heart. Burn away everything that doesn't please You. Revive my soul. Set me on fire again. Let me hunger for Your presence more than anything in this world." In the name of Jesus. Amen!

Prayer for Church Unity

Scriptures Focus:
John 17:21, Ephesians 4:3, Galatians 3:28

"Father, forgive our divisions. Tear down walls between churches, races, and generations. Let us stand as one Body, filled with one Spirit, for one purpose — to lift up Jesus in our city." In the name of Jesus. Amen!

Prayer for the Lost

Scriptures Focus:
Corinthians 4:4, Ezekiel 36:26, Acts 2:21

"Lord, open the eyes of those who are spiritually blind. Let conviction fall and hearts be softened. Draw sons and daughters' home. We declare salvation over every street, home, and neighborhood." In the name of Jesus. Amen!

Sample Prayers for City Revival

Prayer for Youth Awakening

Scriptures Focus:
Joel 2:28, Psalm 110:3

"God, awaken this next generation. Call them by name. Release purpose and fire. Let young people preach, prophesy, and live boldly for You. Mark them with holiness and courage." In the name of Jesus. Amen!

Prayer for City Transformation

Scriptures Focus:
Proverbs 11:11, Jeremiah 29:7, Isaiah 60:18

"Lord Jesus, reign over our city. Let righteousness and justice fill every corner — from city hall to the streets. Bring down corruption. Raise up godly leaders. Let this city be known for revival, not ruin." In the name of Jesus. Amen!

Scripture to Declare:

"Ask of Me, and I will give You the nations for Your inheritance, and the ends of the earth for Your possession."
— Psalm 2:8

Chapter 8

You Are a Revival Carrier

You don't need a microphone, a big stage, or a famous name to spark revival. You just need a **burning heart**, a **willing spirit**, and a **yes** in your soul.

Revival doesn't rest on a few preachers — it spreads through everyday believers who dare to believe that **God can use them**. You are not waiting for revival to come; **revival is waiting for you to release it**.

You are a **carrier of God's glory**, a walking altar, a living flame. Don't underestimate the power of one obedient person surrendered to God.

Your Revival Assignment:
- Pray daily for your city.
- Gather two or three others who are hungry for more.

- Go where the lost are and share Jesus boldly.
- Start small — God will do the rest.
- Keep the fire burning, no matter who shows up or walks away.

Scripture Declaration:

"You are the light of the world. A city on a hill cannot be hidden."
— Matthew 5:14

Chapter 9

Step-by -Step Guide For Revival

Starting a revival in your city is not about hype — it's about hearts ignited by God. True revival starts in the Spirit, flows through yielded people, and transforms families, churches, and even entire communities.

Here's a step-by-step biblical guide to help you become a catalyst for revival in your city:

1. Let Revival Start With You

Revival is personal before it's public. Before a city is changed, your heart must be burning with love for Jesus. Revival doesn't come through talent, strategy, or noise — it comes through personal consecration and hunger for God.

Key Scripture:

"Will You not revive us again, that Your people may rejoice in You?"

— Psalm 85:6

"Search me, O God, and know my heart…"
— Psalm 139:23

2. Build a Prayer Foundation

No revival ever happened without deep, united prayer. Start with one or two others. Set a time.

Intercede for:
- Personal repentance and purity
- The church to awaken
- Your city's leaders, youth, and lost souls

Key Scripture:

"If My people who are called by My name humble themselves, and pray and seek My face and turn from their wicked ways…"
— 2 Chronicles 7:14

"They all joined together constantly in prayer…"
— Acts 1:14

3. Preach the Full Gospel with Power

Revival flourishes where truth is boldly proclaimed and Jesus is lifted high.

Preach:
- Repentance
- The cross
- The power of the Holy Spirit
- Healing, deliverance, and transformation

Let the Word of God cut and heal at the same time.

Key Scripture:

"Faith comes by hearing, and hearing by the word of God."
— Romans 10:17

"You shall receive power after the Holy Spirit has come upon you…"
— Acts 1:8

4. Unite with Other Believers

Revival grows in unity. Reach out to pastors, youth leaders, intercessors, and churches across your city. Start with a few people who are hungry — God will multiply.

Organize:
- United prayer nights
- Worship gatherings
- Community outreach
- Street evangelism

Key Scripture:
"How good and pleasant it is when God's people live together in unity… for there the Lord commands the blessing."
— Psalm 133:1–3

5. Host the Presence of God, Not Just Events

You don't need smoke machines or celebrity speakers — what you need is God's presence.

Make space in your meetings for:

- Deep worship
- Conviction of sin
- The gifts of the Spirit
- Stillness before God

Let God lead the agenda, not the clock.

Key Scripture:
"The Lord is in His holy temple; let all the earth be silent before Him."
— Habakkuk 2:20

6. Take Revival to the Streets

- Revival doesn't stay inside buildings — it overflows into cities. Preach the Gospel in parks, schools, markets, prisons, and neighborhoods. Lay hands on the sick. Feed the poor. Hug the broken.
- Let the city feel the love and power of God in action.

Key Scripture:

"Go into all the world and preach the Gospel…"
— Mark 16:15

7. Disciple the Harvest

Revival is not just about emotions or miracles — it's about lasting fruit. After salvations and deliverances, create:
- Small groups
- Discipleship classes
- Baptism opportunities
- Leadership training

Key Scripture:
"Go and make disciples of all nations…"
— Matthew 28:19

Example: Revival in Acts
The early church model in Acts shows us:
- They prayed continually (Acts 1)
- They were filled with the Spirit (Acts 2)
- They preached boldly (Acts 2–4)
- They cared for the poor (Acts 4:32–35)
- Revival multiplied disciples and shook cities

Final Word: Revival Is God's Work, Not Ours

- You don't need to manufacture it — just make room for it. God sends revival when His people are hungry, holy, and humble.
- "Revival is not churches filled with people, but people filled with God." — Leonard Ravenhill

Chapter 10

Revival Prayer Guide

This Revival Prayer Guide is a powerful tool to stir your heart, unite intercessors, and invite the Spirit of God to move in your city. You can use this as a **daily prayer plan**, a **weekly prayer focus**, or during special **revival prayer gatherings**.

"Lord, send revival, and let it start with me."

DAY 1
Personal Revival

Scripture:

"Search me, O God, and know my heart…"
— *Psalm 139:23*

"Create in me a clean heart, O God…"
— *Psalm 51:10*

Pray:
- Lord, purify my heart. Expose hidden sin.
- Give me a fresh hunger for Your Word and presence.
- Set me on fire again. Let me love what You love and hate what You hate.

Confession:
"I will not settle for cold faith or religious routine. I welcome Your refining fire."

DAY 2
The Church to Awaken

Scripture:

"Wake up, O sleeper, rise from the dead, and Christ will shine on you."
— *Ephesians 5:14*

Pray:
- Lord, awaken every sleeping heart in Your church.
- Revive pastors, worship leaders, youth groups, and elders.
- Remove apathy, division, and worldliness.

Confession:

"The Church is not weak — she is rising with power. Jesus is building His Church."

DAY 3
Repentance and Holiness

Scripture:

"If My people... will humble themselves and pray... and turn from their wicked ways..."
— *2 Chronicles 7:14*

"Be holy, because I am holy."
— *1 Peter 1:16*

Pray:
- Lord, expose sin in our homes, pulpits, and communities.
- Lead us to repentance and true brokenness.
- Restore holiness, purity, and integrity among Your people.

Confession:
"We are a holy people, set apart for Your glory."

DAY 4
Hunger for God's Presence

Scripture:

"Blessed are those who hunger and thirst for righteousness…"
— *Matthew 5:6*

"My soul thirsts for You… in a dry and weary land."
— *Psalm 63:1*

Pray:
- Stir hunger for Your presence in our churches and cities.
- Let worship be passionate, not performance.
- Let Your presence be more desired than programs.

Confession:
"I am hungry for more of You, Lord. Nothing else will satisfy."

DAY 5
Harvest of Souls

Scripture:

"The fields are white unto harvest…"
— *John 4:35*

"He who wins souls is wise."
— *Proverbs 11:30*

Pray:
- Lord, save the lost in our city — from the rich to the poor.
- Open hearts in schools, prisons, streets, and homes.
- Raise up soul winners, evangelists, and witnesses.

Confession:
"My city belongs to Jesus. The harvest is coming in."

DAY 6
The Power of the Holy Spirit

Scripture:

"You shall receive power when the Holy Spirit comes upon you…"
 — *Acts 1:8*

"Not by might, nor by power, but by My Spirit…"
 — *Zechariah 4:6*

Pray:
- Baptize us afresh in the Holy Spirit and fire.
- Let miracles, healings, and signs follow the Gospel.
- Empower us to boldly proclaim Christ.

Confession:
"I walk in the power of the Holy Spirit — not fear, not flesh."

DAY 7
Citywide Transformation

Scripture:

"I have many people in this city."
— *Acts 18:10*

"The city rejoiced with great joy."
— *Acts 8:8*

Pray:
- Lord, transform our city spiritually, socially, and morally.
- Let crime drop, churches fill, and hope rise.
- Place righteous leaders in positions of influence.

Confession:
"My city is a revival center. God's glory will dwell here.

Ongoing Prayer Strategies

- Form **weekly revival prayer groups** in homes or churches.
- Do **prayer walks** through neighborhoods, schools, and city halls.
- Host **worship-and-prayer nights** to saturate the atmosphere
- Fast as the Lord leads (1 meal, 1 day, or more).

Revival Declaration:

"We declare that this is a time of awakening. Our hearts are ready, our prayers are rising, and our city will encounter the glory of God. Lord, send revival — and let it start with us!"

Chapter 11

City Revival Plan

Here's a **step-by-step City Revival Plan** designed to help you stir revival in your city through prayer, unity, outreach, and the presence of God. This plan can be used by churches, small groups, or individuals burdened for their community.

"Lord, send revival — and let it transform our city."

PHASE 1
Personal Preparation
(Week 1–2)

Goal: Start revival in your own heart.

Daily Prayer and Repentance:
- Ask God to search your heart (Psalm 139:23–24).
- Repent of pride, fear, and complacency.
- Surrender your schedule, motives, and influence to God.

Consecrate Yourself:
- Fast for 1–3 days as led by the Holy Spirit.
- Commit to holiness and intimacy with God.

Revival Fire Scriptures:
- Psalm 85:6
- Habakkuk 3:2
- Acts 2
- 2 Chronicles 7:14

PHASE 2
Build the Prayer Network
(Week 2–4)

Goal: Form a revival-focused prayer team across your city.

Gather Intercessors:
- Connect with at least 3–7 people who are hungry for God.
- Start with weekly revival prayer meetings (online or in person).

Launch a Prayer Chain or WhatsApp Group:
- Share daily revival prayer points.
- Encourage city-wide fasting (e.g., 1 day a week).

Prayer Focus Areas:
- Churches to awaken
- Leaders and youth
- Crime and corruption to be broken
- Outpouring of the Holy Spirit

PHASE 3
Unite the Body of Christ
(Month 2)

Goal: Bring churches together to pursue revival in unity.

Reach Out to Pastors and Leaders:
- Host a unity breakfast or prayer fellowship.
- Present a shared vision: not your platform, but God's glory.

Organize City-Wide Prayer Events:
- Joint worship nights
- Outdoor prayer rallies
- Prayer walks in schools, neighborhoods, hospitals

Promote Unity, Not Uniformity:
- Different styles — one Spirit. Respect all tribes of the Body.

Key Verse:
"When the day of Pentecost came, they were all together in one place..."
  — Acts 2:1

PHASE 4
Evangelism and Outreach
(Month 3)

Goal: Share the Gospel and bring people into the Kingdom.

Equip Believers:
- Hold evangelism and spiritual gifts training.
- Prepare your team to preach, pray for the sick, and minister deliverance.

Outreach Opportunities:
- Park outreaches
- School or youth center visits
- Evangelistic crusades or revival nights
- Food and clothing distribution with Gospel prayer booths

Follow Up New Believers:
- Plug them into home churches or small groups.
- Start discipleship classes immediately.

PHASE 5
Sustain the Fire
(Month 4 and Beyond)

Goal: Maintain revival atmosphere and produce lasting fruit.

Weekly Revival Nights:
- Ongoing gatherings for worship, Word, and altar ministry.

Discipleship Pathway:
- Foundations class, Holy Spirit baptism, serving, and evangelism.

Leadership Pipeline:
- Raise up new leaders from the harvest.
- Empower young people and new converts.

Document Testimonies:

- Keep a revival journal or website with powerful stories, miracles, and salvations.
- Share on social media to glorify God.

BONUS
Strategic Revival Tools

Prayer Walking Map:
Mark down schools, police stations, government offices, and crime zones. Pray over each area.

Revival Partnerships:
Partner with ministries, local Christian businesses, youth leaders, and worship teams.

City Declaration:
Print and declare: "This city belongs to Jesus! We declare revival, righteousness, and reformation in every home, every heart, every street!"

Final Word:
Revival doesn't come by force — it comes through **faith, fire, and obedience**. If you stay consistent, God will move. One heart on fire can ignite a city.

"You are the light of the world. A city on a hill cannot be hidden."
— Matthew 5:14

Final Prayer:
"Father, I say yes. I offer You my hands, my voice, my life. Let revival begin in me and spread through me. Use me to shake my generation. I am a revival carrier — for Your glory alone." In the name of Jesus. Amen!

A Prayer For Your City

A Prayer For Your City

Dear Father in heaven, out of *[Insert Name of Your Church]* we pray that people will come to know Jesus, be filled with the Holy Spirit, and that supernatural ministry will take place. We believe that as *[Insert Name of Your Church]* hosts the presence of God, it will produce a perpetual move of the Spirit that will transform and activate gifts in people for the advancement of the kingdom of God, as the Holy Spirit leads.

POSTSCRIPT

If this book has inspired, encouraged, or challenged you in any way, we would love to hear your story. Your testimony is powerful — not only does it bless and encourage me as the author, but it also becomes a light for others who may be walking a similar journey. Whether this book stirred your faith, brought clarity to your calling, or ignited a deeper hunger for God, your testimony matters. Please email us at either email: pa@cityrevive.org or go@cityrevive.org.

You can send a written letter or an email to let us know how this book has touched your heart, shifted your perspective, or produced fruit in your life. Every testimony is a reminder that God's Word never returns void. Your words might be exactly what someone else needs to read one day.

CONNECT

Stay connected with us beyond the pages of this book! We invite you to follow us on Facebook, Threads, and Instagram for encouragement, updates, and behind-the-scenes glimpses of what God is doing through this ministry. Be sure to subscribe to our YouTube channel, where you'll find powerful teachings, testimonies, and uplifting content designed to strengthen your walk with Christ.

To learn more about our vision, mission, and how you can be part of what God is building, visit our website at cityrevive. Visit wordnspirit.tv to watch life-changing messages that will equip and empower you to live in the fullness of God's Spirit. We're honored to walk this journey with you!

CONNECT

Facebook: facebook.com/drstevembua

Instagram: @drstevembua

TikTok: @drstevembua

Youtube: @cityrevive

Website: cityrevive.org

To Give: cityrevive.org/give

Video On Demand: wordnspirit.tv

About the Author

Dr. Steve Mbua is a passionate voice for revival, faith, and Kingdom leadership. His heart burns to see believers awakened, cities transformed, and Jesus glorified in every sphere of life. Through preaching, writing, and mentoring, he empowers people to walk in their divine calling and make lasting impact.

Notes

Notes

Made in the USA
Columbia, SC
20 June 2025